Editor: Penny Clarke
Consultant: Henrietta McCall

JOHN MALAM
studied ancient history and archaeology at the University of Birmingham, after which
he worked as an archaeologist at the Ironbridge Gorge Museum, Shropshire. He is
now an author, specializing in information books for children. He lives in Cheshire
with his wife, a book designer, and their two children.

HENRIETTA McCALL
studied ancient history as part of her degree at Oxford University. She has edited a
number of children's books set in antiquity and written a book on Mesopotamian
myths published by the British Museum. She contributed to the *British Museum's
Book of Mythical Beasts* and to *The Legacy of Mesopotamia* published by Oxford
University Press in 1998.

DAVID ANTRAM
was born in Brighton in 1958. He studied at Eastbourne College of Art and then
worked in advertising for fifteen years. He lives in Sussex with his wife and two
children.

DAVID SALARIYA
studied illustration and printmaking in Dundee, Scotland. He has created a range of
books for publishers in the UK and overseas, including the award-winning *Very
Peculiar History* series. In 1989 he established The Salariya Book Company. He lives
in Brighton with his wife, the illustrator Shirley Willis, and their son Jonathan.

Created, designed, and produced by
The SALARIYA BOOK CO. LTD
25 Marlborough Place
Brighton BN1 1UB

First published in 1999 by Franklin Watts

First American edition 1999 by Franklin Watts/Children's Press
A Division of Grolier Publishing
90 Sherman Turnpike
Danbury CT 06816

Visit Franklin Watts/Children's Press on the Internet at:
http//publishing.grolier.com

Library of Congress Cataloging-in-Publication Data
Malam, John
    Ancient Greek Town/written by John Malam: illustrated by David Antram.
        p. cm. – – (Metropolis)
    Includes index.
    Summary: Presents life in a town in ancient Greece, covering the temple, town square,
a family home, an open-air theater, games, the cemetery, the port, and more.
        ISBN 0–531–14529–8 (Hardback)
            0–531–15379–7 (Paperback)
    1. Cities and towns, Ancient– –Greece– –Pictorial works– –Juvenile literature. 2.
Greece—Civilization—To 146 B.C.—Juvenile
literature. [1. Greece—Civilization—To 146 B.C.] I. Antram, David, 1958– ill. II.Title. III. Series; Metropolis
(Franklin Watts, inc.)
DF78.M27 1999   98–41945
938—dc21   CIP
                                                                                     AC

GROLIER
PUBLISHING

Printed in Singapore.

METROPOLIS

GREEK TOWN

Written by John Malam

Illustrated by David Antram

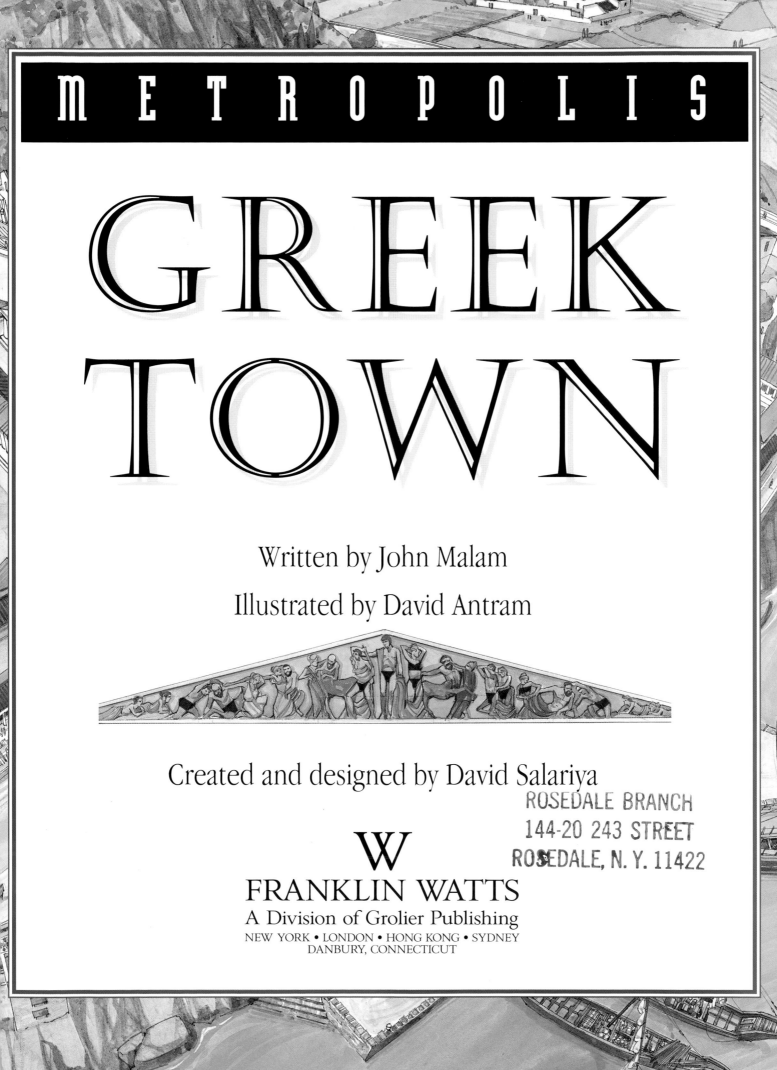

Created and designed by David Salariya

W
FRANKLIN WATTS
A Division of Grolier Publishing
NEW YORK • LONDON • HONG KONG • SYDNEY
DANBURY, CONNECTICUT

Contents

INTRODUCTION

Situated at the eastern end of the Mediterranean Sea is the land of Greece. The Romans called it "Graecia," and it is from this Latin word that the name "Greece" comes. It is a rugged place, with mountains covering almost three-quarters of the land. They line up in long ranges, between which are fertile valleys where rivers flow. It has been said that the mountain ranges make Greece seem like a country with all its ribs showing. Beyond the mainland are some 2,000 islands, large and small, scattered like stepping-stones in the clear blue water westward as far as the shores of Turkey. Fewer than 200 of the islands are inhabited – most are barren, rocky places. This was the landscape the ancient Greeks knew, some 2,500 years ago.

The civilization of the ancient Greeks was at its most glorious between about 500 B.C. and 300 B.C. It was a time of great discoveries in science, mathematics, and medicine, a time when many famous politicians, architects, sculptors, philosophers, dramatists, and historians lived. Cities, towns, and villages were spread throughout Greece, the greatest of which was the city of Athens.

In this book we take you on a tour of a Greek town as it was in about 400 B.C. It is a town built close to the sea, like so many others on the mainland of Greece. You will find that it is enjoying a period of prosperity. Its streets are lined with fine new buildings in the latest styles; merchants come here to trade; athletes from all of Greece compete at the festival of games; pilgrims offer gifts to the gods at the temple; and the sick seek cures at the sanctuary. Since the ending of the war against Persia, the old enemy of Greece, the town's inhabitants have never had it so good. In this time of peace, their town has become a rich and beautiful place.

Around the Town

The Sacred Sanctuary

Feeling ill? Then go to the sanctuary on pages 28 and 29, where healers will tell you how you can be cured. You'll need to take a sheep as an offering to the sanctuary god.

The Cemetery

The dead are laid to rest outside the city – but will their souls travel to the Elysian Fields, to lead a life of happiness, or to Tartarus and a life of torment? Find out on pages 30 and 31.

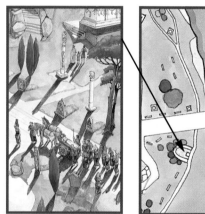

Craftworkers' Quarter

Everywhere you go you will see the handiwork of the town's craftspeople. Learn the trade secrets of making clay into pottery, stone into statues, and metal into jewelry on pages 18 and 19.

The Town Square

The town center is packed with traders and people holding meetings. Join them on pages 16 and 17.

Games and Festivals

The games are the most exciting event in town. What sports do athletes compete in? Be there with the crowds on pages 24 and 25.

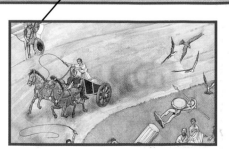

The Temple

Why do people go to the temple on the hill above the town? What do they see inside? What goes on at the altar in the sacred enclosure? Join the faithful on pages 14 and 15.

A Farm in the Country

Farmers in the country grow food to feed the town's population. What crops do they grow? What animals do they keep? How is wine made? Discover the farming year on pages 32 and 33.

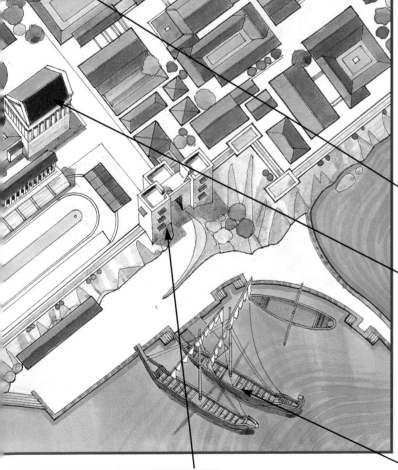

A Family Home

What is a Greek town house like? On pages 20 and 21 you'll discover what goes on inside the home of an ordinary family and what you can expect to eat if you're invited to a meal.

Open-Air Theater

Set in a hollow in the side of a hill, the theater is the place to see comedies, tragedies, and histories. But why do the actors wear masks? And where should you sit? Be entertained on pages 22 and 23.

The Council-house

Who are the members of the town council? What do they discuss inside the council-house? Find out about this important public building on pages 12 and 13.

Town Walls and Defenses

The town is surrounded by a stone wall. Who does it keep out? What weapons do Greek soldiers use? Go to pages 26 and 27 to find out about the Greeks at war.

The Port and Harbor

It is said that the Greeks live around the sea like frogs around a pond. Why is the sea so important? When is it safest to travel by boat? Begin your voyage on pages 34 and 35.

THE COUNCIL-HOUSE

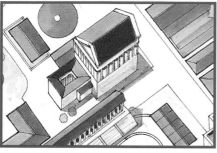

The council-house is where the town's elected officials hold their meetings. It is a major public building in a prominent position in the center of town. Its interior can be compared with the town's open-air theater: it too has tiers of stone seats that surround a central area, and everyone has a clear view of the speaker who addresses his audience as if he were an actor. As many as 500 councillors attend meetings, which are held on most days of the year. They decide how the town and its territory are to be run – especially how much money needs to be collected in taxes, and how it should be spent. Council meetings are often very noisy, and councillors do not always pay attention to what the speaker says. When it is time to vote, councillors raise their hands to be counted.

Male citizens aged over 18 can vote in the Assembly. These meetings decide whether to declare war or make peace. It is government by the people for the people.

A fragment of pottery used in a vote of ostracism, on which is scratched the name "Aristides, son of Lysimachus."

Only men aged over 30 can be members of the Council. They must be citizens of the town – those born outside town cannot be elected. At meetings they wear wreaths made from leaves of myrtle. The wreaths are religious emblems.

Once a year in the spring, each male citizen has the chance to send a person into exile – usually an unpopular politician. A ballot is held in the town square. Voters scratch the name of the person they wish to see banished onto pieces of pottery, called ostraka, from which comes our word "ostracize" (banish). They throw them into a large urn. The person with the most votes is ostracized. He must leave town within ten days – and not return for ten years.

THE TEMPLE

Animal sacrifices please the gods. A priest leads the way to the altar, followed by the person who is offering a sheep for sacrifice. Musicians go with them. On the priest's tray are utensils for the sacrifice.

Altar

O n the hill above town is the temple. It is the home of the sacred spirit who watches over and protects the town and its people. Each town worships its own favorite god or goddess – such as Athena, the goddess of war, wisdom, and art who is worshiped here. Her statue, made from ivory, gold, and wood, stands in the main room of the temple. People are welcome to enter the temple, where they may leave gifts of food for the goddess. Outside is the sacred enclosure, where priests sacrifice animals. Their blood is splashed onto the altar, and the goddess feeds upon it. Their bones and internal organs are burned on the altar fire. Then their meat is cooked and eaten. A bull is the greatest gift you can give the goddess; a sheep is the most common.

Statue of the goddess Athena

1   2   3

The temple's columns seem straight (1), but this is an optical illusion. If they were straight they would actually look crooked (2). So they are built on a curved base and lean inward (3).Columns are carved in different styles. Here it is the Doric style. Each column is made up of sections or drums. Grooves, or flutes, are cut down each column.

Corinthian column

Doric column

Ionic column

Painted statues adorn each end of the temple. This one shows centaurs – creatures that are part human, part horse.

THE TOWN SQUARE

An official checks that a stallholder is not cheating. He makes sure the trader's weights measure the correct amount. If they do not, the trader is banned.

The town square, or agora, is a large open area. It is put to many uses. Traders set up market stalls, covered with sun-shades. They sell fresh fruit and vegetables grown on their farms. Around the edge of the square are long, low buildings with open fronts, called stoas. They are covered walkways, with shops at the back. Elsewhere in the square are fountains, from which drinking water pours. It comes from an underground spring. No one has running water at home, so people collect it at the fountains. Sometimes the square is used for a meeting of the citizens' Assembly. They listen to a speaker, and then vote on what he has been saying. At other times, trials are held here.

The town uses its own silver and gold coins. Traders only accept coins made in town. They do not take "foreign" coins from other towns.

A stoa provides shade from the sun. Some people come here to talk about religion. They are the ones who believe in only one god. Since they meet in the stoa, they are called Stoics.

When a speaker talks to a group of citizens, he has a set time for his speech. He must stop when all the water has drained from a water clock.

At a trial, jurors give their verdict with two bronze discs. One has a hollow center and means "guilty"; the other has a solid center and means "not guilty." Jurors put one into a metal box, the other into a wooden box. Only the discs in the metal box are counted.

Water clock

CRAFTWORKERS' QUARTER

Tucked away behind the town square is the craftworkers' quarter, where skilled makers and artists turn clay, stone, bone, ivory, glass, leather, wood, and metal into a great variety of objects. Their workshops are filled with the noise of saw on wood, chisel on stone, hammer on iron, and the roar of the fiery furnace. The potters' workshop is like a small factory, where groups of men work hard to keep up with the never-ending demand for their wares. Most popular of all are tall vases called amphorae, meaning "two-handled." These are used for storing wine, honey, olives, and grapes.

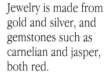

Pottery vases are painted with scenes of black or red figures from myths. The painter often signs his name.

The tall loutrophoros (far left) holds water at weddings and funerals. A lekythos holds oil.

A kylix, or wine cup. Its shallow bowl is easy to drink from while reclining.

Kraters are the large vessels in which wine and water are mixed at meals.

A kantharos is a wine cup used at the table.

Jewelry is made from gold and silver, and gemstones such as carnelian and jasper, both red.

Blacksmiths forge iron by heating and hammering it into shape. They use it to make sharp-edged tools such as axes and swords.

Marble block is dragged to the workshop.

In the marble quarry outside town, slaves knock wooden wedges into slots in the marble. These expand when water is poured over them, breaking a block free.

A Family Home

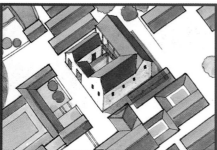

A man's tunic is called a chiton.

A Greek home turns its back on the town. Its plain white walls have few windows, and unless you are invited inside, then what lies beyond will remain private – out of sight from the prying eyes of passers-by. But go through the entrance gates and you enter an open courtyard, where there is an altar to the god of the household. Rooms surround the courtyard. Here there is also a storeroom containing supplies of food, which servants prepare in the kitchen. They serve food to the family and their guests in the andron, or dining room. At a banquet, people eat the food as they recline on couches. The upper floor is reached by a staircase from the courtyard. Here are bedrooms and a workroom, where women weave cloth on looms.

Stone or clay loomweights keep the threads taut.

A woman wears a one-piece tunic called a peplos, made from undyed wool or linen. It is held by a belt at the waist. Women spend much time at home, weaving all the cloth the family needs.

Outside the home a man wears leather sandals. He goes barefoot indoors.

Children play with spinning tops, dolls, and models of carts. In the street they have fun with hoops.

Spinning top

One of the town's potters has made a new type of vessel from clay. It's a potty for young children!

Guests who stay for a meal will eat good food. There may be fish and eels, or even quails (small birds) cooked in garlic sauce, all served with fresh vegetables. Fruit, nuts, and cheese will follow, washed down with cups of wine.

Open-Air Theater

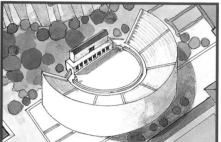

Tragic actor   Comic actor

Most towns have an open-air theater. Many, like the one here, occupy an area of flat ground with the seats around a bowl-shaped hollow. This is the ideal shape for a theater. It allows actors' voices to carry to the farthest seats, while everyone in the audience has a clear view of the performance. The best seats are in the front row. They look like armchairs and are for important people. Other people sit on the tiers of uncomfortable stone seats that rise up behind. Plays are performed in the daytime by actors who speak or sing their parts. They act on a circular area of beaten earth, called the orchestra.

Theater tickets are in the form of bronze discs. Each has a letter on it to indicate in which kerkis, or block of seats, the ticket-holder is to sit.

A play is accompanied by music. The lura, or lyre, is a stringed instrument plucked with the fingers of one hand. It makes a gentle sound. Shrill, exciting music is made by the aulos, a wind instrument like a flute that can be played two at a time.

Lyres have 7 to 12 strings.

To play two aulos, the musician straps two to his head.

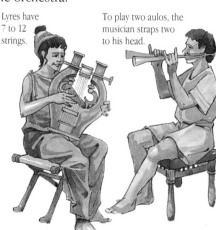

Actors wear masks of wood, cork, or linen. The masks' expressions show if it is a sad (tragic) or happy (comic) part. Padded clothes and thick-soled shoes form the rest of the costume.

The ekkyklema, or "wheel-out," is a platform on wheels. The victim lies on it, while the murderer stands over the body.

If a play calls for an actor to fly through the air, a mechane, or crane, is used to hoist him aloft. In *The Birds*, a play by Aristophanes, two actors create a bird city in the sky, called Cloud-Cuckoo-Land. Stagehands operate the crane out of sight of the audience.

Crane's lifting arm

AT THE GAMES

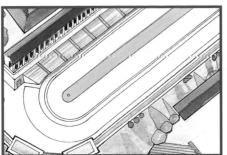

When the town holds its festival of games, athletes come from all over Greece to compete in the five-day program of events. The organizers want the festival to be the best there is, so that people will think highly of the town. The horse track, or hippodrome, is a place of great excitement when chariots race around it. Crashes are frequent because the turns at each end are very tight.

Throwing the discus

A thrower makes a three-quarter turn of his body before he lets go of the 5.5lb (2.5kg) bronze discus.

The discus can be thrown 98 ft (30 m).

A 5lb (2.3kg) stone weight, or halter, used in the long jump.

In the long jump, athletes jump from a standing start. They swing two weights to help them go farther.

The race-in-armor, or hoplitodromos, is for runners who race in their helmets while carrying shields.

Acrobats on stilts and horseback, jugglers, and musicians entertain the crowd. Pedlars sell lucky charms, and farmers bring baskets of fruit.

A winning athlete is presented with a crown of olive branches and a palm frond. Victory ribbons are tied to his upper arms.

Town Defenses

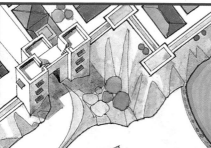

A high wall built from large blocks of well-fitting stone surrounds the town. The wall is quite new. In times of trouble in the past, the town's inhabitants took shelter on the hill, or acropolis, above the town, where the temple stands. But now that the wall has been built, the town is a stronger place. People know that an enemy army will not find it quite so easy to invade the town. They will be able to withstand a siege, until, with luck, the enemy is forced to abandon the attack. However, if they do take the town, knocking down the wall, its towers, and its gateways will be the first thing the invaders will do.

A hoplite's helmet is made from a sheet of bronze, beaten into shape. A crest of colored horsehair decorates the top. When not fighting, hoplites push their helmets away from their faces.

Persian soldiers wore loose clothing and soft caps. They fought with spears, swords, and bows and arrows.

Wicker shield covered with animal hide.

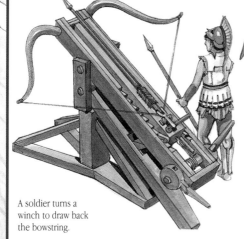

A soldier turns a winch to draw back the bowstring.

Catapults on the town's walls shoot 6.5-ft (2-m)-long arrows. The arrows' iron tips pierce armor, which is why arrows are called katapeltes, or shield-piercers.

Foot soldiers in the Greek army are called hoplites, from their hoplons, or shields. They fight with spears, but if these break, they use their swords.

The Persians are old enemies of the Greeks. Although there is now an uneasy peace between the two sides, neither really trusts the other.

THE SACRED SANCTUARY

Outside town, among a grove of cypress trees, is the sanctuary. It is visited by the sick, who come from all over Greece. They bring sacrifices to offer Asclepius, the god of healing. This is his special place, where cures are sought. The snake is his symbol, and many live inside his temple.

First an attendant washes the body of a pilgrim in the sacred pool. Then the blood of a sheep is spilled at an altar, after which the person sleeps in a cell at the back of a stoa. They hope to have a dream in which Asclepius visits them. Next morning, inside the temple, the god's priests interpret the dream, telling the worshiper how he or she is to be cured. Whey they leave the sanctuary, visitors put small gifts of food on an altar, as a "thank you" to the god for curing them.

Inside the stoa, which is like a dormitory, the sick person sleeps on the fleece of a sacrificed sheep. Asclepius comes to them in a dream.

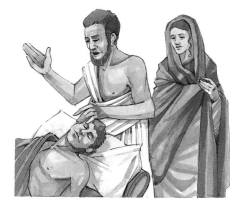

The dream can only be understood by a priest, who explains what it means.

A pilgrim can talk to the gods through a priestess who goes into a trance. In answer to a question, she utters strange words. A priest makes sense of them as he writes them down.

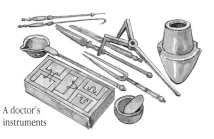

A doctor's instruments

Doctors are thought of as craftsmen. They use surgical instruments and medicines made from herbs to cure illnesses.

THE CEMETERY

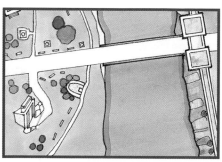

Burial within the town is forbidden, so the cemetery is along a road, beyond a gateway into the town. There is a mixture of tombs. Simple ones are cut into the rock; others are grand monuments called mausolea. A funeral takes place at sunrise. The procession is led by a woman with a vase. It contains oils and perfumes to be sprinkled at the graveside. A cart carries the body, head first, to the grave. It is dressed in white, and the face is uncovered. Mourners in black walk behind, men before women. The women beat their chests and wail, and one has shaved her head to show she is in mourning. Musicians follow the party. If the dead person has been murdered, the chief mourner carries a spear. At the tomb the body is put into a stone coffin, surrounded by food and objects for use in the next life.

A stone slab, called a stele, marks the place of the grave.

THE JOURNEY TO THE UNDERWORLD

1. Hermes, the gods' messenger, leads the dead person to the River Styx.

2. Charon, the ferryman, rows him across the river — but only if he can pay the fare.

3. Cerberus, the three-headed dog, guards the entrance to the Underworld. The dead need only worry if they try to leave, as Cerberus will stop them.

4. Those who have led good lives are let into the Elysian Fields, a place of happiness.

5. But those who have led bad lives are sent to Tartarus, a place of punishment where their souls will never rest in peace.

A Farm in the Country

Farming is the main activity of the Greek world, and farmers are highly thought of, as it is their job to feed the people. There are many farms around town, growing a wide variety of foods to send to market. Wheat and barley are the main cereals grown, from which bread and cakes are made. Olives and grapes are the main fruit crops, but apples, pears, figs, and pomegranates are also grown. Vegetables include peas, leeks, onions, beans, and lettuces. Sheep, goats, pigs, and cattle are kept. Crops are grown in small fields. The soil is thin and stony, and it is difficult to plow. Stones cleared off the land are used to build field walls. Many farmers keep hives of bees, from which they collect honey, used to sweeten food.

The hills around the town are rich with wildlife. Hunters and their dogs go in search of prey, especially wild boar. They also trap birds in nets strung between trees.

The olive harvest begins in November, but the trees will go on producing fruit until February. The branches of the trees are hit with sticks, and the falling olives are caught in nets spread out below. Most are crushed for their oil. It is used for cooking, as fuel for lamps, and in religious ceremonies. Olives can be eaten both when they are green and unripe or black and ripe.

MAKING WINE

1. Grapes grow well on the hills around town. They ripen during the long, hot summer and are picked in September.

2. The grapes are put in vats. Workers stomp on them to squeeze out the juice. Presses squeeze the last drops from the pulp.

3. The juice is stored in jars for six months. This is its fermenting time, when alcohol forms from natural sugars in the juice.

4. By March, the juice has become wine, and it is poured into smaller jars. Sieves catch the grape skins and other bits.

5. Greek wine is strong and sweet. It is drunk mixed with water – two parts water to one part wine is best.

THE PORT AND HARBOR

A trireme is a warship rowed by many oarsmen. A bronze battering ram on the bow helps it ram enemy ships.

The trireme's rowers sit in three rows, one above the other. Stones in the bottom of the ship give it stability.

Ships sail into the sheltered harbor from all parts of the Mediterranean. Merchant ships bring goods from the distant lands of Africa and Asia. Some even trade with barbarian tribes far to the north, at the very edge of the world. Greek traders want their metals, such as tin and lead. Fishing boats unload the day's catch, as noisy seabirds fight for scraps thrown overboard by the fishermen. Some boats bring sponges, too, picked from the seabed by divers who can hold their breath for three or four minutes. Travelers who come by sea do so when it is calm: the best time is between May and September.

Firelight from the lighthouse turns night into day. Ships sail home safely, guided by its light.

A "ship shaker" keeps the port safe from attack. Its giant claw can be swung under an enemy ship.

As a team of oxen pull on a rope, the shaker's arm lifts up, raising the ship's bow out of the sea.

When it has been lifted as high as it can go, the rope is released, and the ship crashes down.

GOODS BROUGHT IN BY SHIP

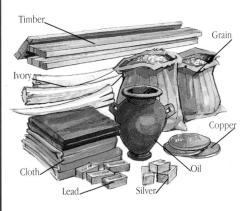

Timber

Grain

Ivory

Cloth

Lead

Silver

Oil

Copper

Greek owners, who buy slaves at the slave market at the port, think of them as "living tools." Male slaves are bought to do heavy work in quarries. Female slaves do house-work. Children make good slaves because they can be trained for a long life of slavery.

TIME-TRAVELER'S GUIDE

TRAVEL AND CLIMATE

Most travelers come to Greece by sea. Coastal towns and villages have safe harbors where a ship may moor for a few days, or take shelter while a storm passes by. If you are sailing at night, look for lights burning in lighthouses – they will guide you to safety and warn you away from dangerous rocks.

Pirates are another danger of the sea, particularly around the island of Delos, which has become their base. They raid ships in search of valuables – and to take prisoners to sell in the slave markets of Delos.

Donkeys are the main means of transport for travelers on land. They are perfectly suited to the rocky landscape and can carry a visitor and his bags high into the hills.

The weather in summer is nearly always hot and dry, and temperatures reach 78°F (26°C). Winters are often cold and damp, with temperatures seldom higher than 50°F (10°C). Snow falls in the mountains, cutting off some towns and villages for days.

WHAT TO WEAR

Clothes are simple and loose-fitting. They are cool to wear and comfortable to travel in. Most are made from undyed wool or linen and are a distinctive creamy color.

The basic item of clothing for both men and women is the sleeveless tunic. A women's belted tunic, or peplos, is worn long and reaches the ground. A man wears a shorter tunic, or chiton, which is easy for him to work in. A woolen cloak, the chlamus, is worn for horse riding, but only men wear them because only men ride horses.

Hats with broad rims, called petasos, protect the wearer from the sun. Open-toed leather sandals are worn outdoors. They are suitable for short walks, but a traveler planning a longer trip should wear calf-length lace-up walking boots. Shoes are not usually worn in houses.

Women keep their hair long, but not slaves, who tend to have short cuts. Ribbons are used to tie hair up. Men keep their hair short and many of them grow beards.

WHAT TO EAT AND DRINK

You will be pleasantly surprised at the wide choice of good food and drink available in all parts of Greece. Breakfast is a light meal of bread dipped in wine. Similar food is eaten for lunch, but with cheese and fruit. The main meal is eaten in the evening. It often consists of a first course of fish and vegetables, followed by fruit and honey cakes. In winter, when fishermen do not venture out to sea every day, a hot barley porridge is the main food eaten. It is thick and extremely filling.

Food is served on pottery or wooden plates and bowls and is eaten with fingers and spoons. Wine is drunk from shallow cups.

Men may be invited to a symposium – a party that means "drinking together." Women cannot attend. Guests lie on couches and indulge in conversations about politics, while drinking great quantities of wine. At the end of the party they may walk through town in a noisy torchlight procession known as a komos.

TIME-TRAVELER'S GUIDE

THE GREEK LANGUAGE

Visitors will hear many dialects spoken in rural, isolated parts of the country and on the islands. However, changes are starting to happen to the language in towns and cities. Here, local dialects are disappearing in favor of the koine, or common language. This version of Greek will soon be spoken all over the land, and those who speak it will be understood wherever they go. A few useful words and phrases to know are:

HELLO / GOODBYE
CHAIRE (*say:* khy-re)

THANK YOU
CHARIN ECHO (*say:* khar-in ek-o)

YES
NAI (*say:* ny)

NO
OUCHI (*say:* ook-hi)

HOW MUCH?
POSOU (*say:* poss-oo)

WHERE?
POU (*say:* poo)

WHEN?
POTE (*say:* po-tay)

HAVE YOU ANY FOOD?
TI SITOU EXETE
(*say:* tee sit-oo ex-et-ay)

It helps to know some words, so practice these for your trip.

MONEY

Most coins are made of silver or copper. A few are made of gold. At first, travelers may find the system of Greek coinage a little confusing. This is because each town mints its own coins, which are to be spent only in that town. Coins from other towns will not be accepted.

It is advisable for travelers to exchange coins from other towns with a money changer. Look for him in the town square. He will take your "foreign" money, weigh it on small scales, then exchange it for the local currency. Greek coins contain a fixed amount of metal, and by weighing them the money changer will know how much your "foreign" coins are worth in the local money.

The drachma and the obol are two common coins. Most people earn about half a drachma a day.

1 OBOL = 1/6 DRACHMA
1 HALF OBOL = 1/12 DRACHMA
1 HEMIDRACHMA = 1/2 DRACHMA
1 DRACHMA = 1 DRACHMA
1 DIDRACHMA = 2 DRACHMAS
1 OCTADRACHMA = 8 DRACHMAS
1 DECADRACHMA = 10 DRACHMAS
1 DODECADRACHMA = 12 DRACHMAS

WHERE TO STAY

Greek hospitality is well known, and finding a place to stay in town will not be difficult. Owners of some of the larger town houses have guest rooms where they will gladly let you stay, in return for a small payment.

While you are a guest of a citizen of the town, observe their customs and beliefs, even if they are different from your own. For example, it is always diplomatic for a guest to leave a small offering of food at the altar to the god of the house. Your host will appreciate your gift, as it will show that you respect his god.

You can expect your room to be sparsely furnished. Apart from a chair, a bed, and a chest in which you should store your belongings, there may be little else there. But remember, as you may only be there for a night or two, this is all you will need for a comfortable and relaxing stay before you continue your travels.

Break-ins do happen, especially from wall diggers, or toichorychoi, who burrow through soft walls of mud brick. Do not leave anything you value unattended in your room.

TIME-TRAVELER'S GUIDE

FESTIVAL OF GAMES

If your visit is in August or September, you may find the town's five-day festival of games is being staged. The usual program of events is:

DAY 1
opening ceremony
public and private sacrifices
boys' running, wrestling, and boxing contests

DAY 2
chariot races
horse races
pentathlon (running, discus, jumping, javelin, wrestling)
parade of winners
singing of hymns

DAY 3
the main sacrifices
foot races
public banquet

DAY 4
wrestling
boxing
"pankration" (boxing, kicking, and wrestling combined)
race-in-armor

DAY 5
winners receive their wreaths
closing ceremony
feasting

Don't worry if your visit is at another time, as festivals are held throughout the year.

LOCAL CUSTOMS

Many towns have their own local customs, which to an outsider can seem strange and a little mysterious.

Chief among these so-called "mystery cults" is the worship of the god Dionysus. He is the god of wine and his followers believe they can speak directly to him – but only after they have danced and drunk themselves into a state of excitement known as ekstasis, or ecstasy. They may even eat raw meat as part of their frenzy.

Those who work themselves up into this state say that it feels as if Dionysus actually enters their bodies, replacing their minds with his.

Followers of Dionysus are looking for a way to be reborn into the world. They believe that he has the power to grant them total happiness on earth.

Unwary travelers should exercise caution if a follower of the cult of Dionysus invites them to a party. It will doubtless involve consuming a great deal of alcohol, without any guarantee that Dionysus will appear to the visitor – the appearance of a bad headache the next day is much more likely. Think before you drink!

SHOPPING FOR SOUVENIRS

The town square is the best place for souvenirs. Most traders will accept coins. Do remember that you must use the town's own coins if you want to buy goods. Some traders may be willing to barter with you, swapping their goods for some of yours. However, as this is now an old-fashioned method of exchange, you may find that bartering is practiced only in the more backward parts of Greece, where coins are still not used.

Choose your souvenirs with care. Although pottery can be inexpensive, it is easily broken if not well wrapped for your return journey. If you do buy a pot, ask the seller to pack plenty of straw around it. Look for an unusual pot such as a wine cooler. Its double walls hold a filling of ice to chill your favorite wine.

Textiles also make good souvenirs. Exotic silks from Asia may be too expensive for most travelers, but locally woven woolens and linens are much more affordable.

For those who prefer edible souvenirs, a jar of olives will give them a taste of Greece for many months to come.

TIME-TRAVELER'S GUIDE

STREET ENTERTAINERS

Wherever you travel, you are bound to come across the song-stitchers, or rhapsoidoi. Town squares are their favorite meeting places, where they can be sure that a crowd of people will quickly gather to hear their tale.

Take time to stop and listen as a storyteller entertains a crowd with tales about kings and heroes, monsters and magic. He speaks clearly, raising and lowering his voice in a rhythm that makes the story flow like poetry.

The story will be long, and the crowd will not want the rhapsode to leave any of it out. If he is telling a well-known story, such as the one about the Minotaur monster that lived in the labyrinth at the palace of King Minos, or the one about Daedalus and Icarus who flew like the birds, then the crowd will probably know it already. So, to hold their attention, the bard will add in new details – he will literally "stitch" the story together in a way that will keep the crowd entertained.

And when the storyteller has finished, it is always good to offer him a small coin.

DOCTORS AND MEDICINE

Should you get sick on your visit, you will be in safe hands if you visit one of the new types of doctors who is a follower of Hippocrates, the "Father of Medicine." These doctors keep the Hippocratic Oath, the main part of which says they will never treat patients for any purpose other than to heal them.

Hippocrates said: "We diagnose sickness by observing habits, diet, age and work. One should also take into account sweating, cold, shivering, coughing, sneezing, hiccuping, breathing, belching, and passing wind."

After a doctor has made a diagnosis, he will prescribe a cure. Often this will be in the form of a medicine made from herbs. Eye complaints can be cured with saffron, and fennel is good for calming the nerves. Mustard infused in cucumber sauce is used for fits.

More severe conditions can be made better by cupping, where heated metal cups applied to the patient's body draw off the fluids causing the problem. If this fails, the doctor may resort to bleeding the patient with leeches.

GOOD MANNERS

Visitors should be on their best behavior while they are in town. The Greeks will be as interested in your manners and general conduct as you will be in theirs.

When you greet a person, it is customary to shake their hand and offer a few words of good luck, such as "Work and prosper," or "May your efforts bring success."

If you are invited into a person's house, be prepared for them to ask you to remove your outdoor shoes. You may be offered slippers to wear while you are inside.

If you are asked to a meal, you should accept, as to refuse will cause offense to the host, who likes to dine with company. At the meal, show respect for the god of the house by offering a small gift of wine or food at the altar. If the meal is a banquet, expect to eat it as you recline on a low couch. Do not be surprised if another guest wishes to share the couch with you – it should be big enough for the two of you. As the meal may last for several hours, it is not considered rude if guests take short naps between courses.

GUIDED TOURS

TO THE VISITOR . . .

A new town can seem a strange place to the visitor, especially one from the quiet of the country who is not used to the noise of crowds and a confusing maze of streets. These tours will help visitors find their way around – follow the suggestions and you will soon feel at home. For a visitor "bitten by the travel bug," some of Greece's ever-popular tourist centers are also described here.

WALK THE WALL

V isitors are welcome to walk around the town wall. To walk the entire circuit, start at sunrise and aim to finish before midday, since walking in the afternoon heat can be uncomfortable. In the clear light of early morning you will see far into the distance. Watch fishing boats returning to harbor, then look across the countryside at farms dotted among the hills. The sound of bells, worn by sheep and goats on their collars, will fill the air, and scents from flowers and herbs will smell like the perfume of the gods. After this walk, seek out the shade of a stoa in the town square.

TOWN SQUARE

T he town square is a good place to meet friends, as streets lead to it from all directions. Choose a meeting place carefully. It might seem like a good idea to meet at a trader's stall, but there is no guarantee the trader will be there at the time you want to meet your friend! A stoa is a good place to meet, especially on a hot day when it provides shade from the glare of the sun.

The square is the living heart of the town. It is the center of social life, business, and politics. It can also be a rough and vulgar place, the haunt of gossips and pickpockets.

Note the many statues and altars that stand in the square. You may also witness a meeting of the citizens' Assembly. Listen to the speaker as he addresses the crowd, then watch as they vote for or against his proposal.

From the square, walk across to the council-house.

COUNCIL-HOUSE

S ituated in a corner of the town square is the council-house, or bouleuterion. You can be certain of seeing a meeting in progress as councillors meet here most days. They decide what should be discussed at the next meeting of the Assembly.

If you wish to observe the council at work, please do so quietly from the gangway that runs behind the top tier of seats. Leave when asked to.

A FOUNTAIN-HOUSE

F rom the council-house, return to the town square to collect drinking water from a fountain-house. As fresh water is scarce, it is good to carry some with you – particularly if you plan on visiting the countryside.

Water carriers made from pottery or leather can be bought from traders in the square. Check them for cracks or holes before parting with your money.

The sweetest water is from the Enneakrounos fountain-house, where water continually spurts from nine spouts. Be prepared to wait in line until it is your turn to collect water at this ever-popular source.

GUIDED TOURS

TEMPLE

A road from the square leads past craftworkers' buildings and on to the main temple. Built on the hill that overlooks the town, the temple dominates the surroundings. Not surprisingly, it can be seen from miles around.

The climb up is steep, and visitors should take care during the final part of the ascent. The rock over which you will walk has been polished smooth by the passage of thousands of pairs of feet, and it is now shiny white and quite slippery.

An imposing gateway, looking for all the world like a temple itself, marks the entrance to the temenos, or sacred enclosure. As you follow the well-worn route to the temple, you will hear the sound of religious music. The air will be thick with the strong smell of offerings, which burn on the altar fire. The altar lies at the eastern end of the temple.

Inside the temple is the great gold and ivory statue of Athena, to whom the temple is dedicated. Her gaze is fixed on the altar. She watches as her priests sacrifice sheep to please her, then toss their carcasses to burn on the fire.

To please Athena, place a gift at her altar before you leave.

HARBOR

The cool breeze blowing in from the sea will be a welcome relief as you descend from the sticky heat of the hill on which the temple stands. Follow the main road that takes you past the town square, which is on your right, and you will soon come to a gateway in the town wall. Walk through, then on down the hill to the harbor.

It can seem a world away from the town. Ships bring goods from the Greek colonies of Massilia *(Marseilles, in France)*, Neapolis *(which means New Town and is better known as Naples, in Italy)*, Syracuse *(on Sicily)*, Odessos *(Odessa, in Ukraine)*, and Naukratis *(Kom Gi'eif, in Egypt)*.

Nearby is a place where you'll see ships being built – Greek shipwrights are the best, and Greek ships rule the seas.

You'll be able to buy fresh fish, octopus, and squid as the harvest of the sea is unloaded.

THEATER

Feel like seeing a play? Then go back along the main road through town and take the last turn right, which leads straight to the theatrum, which means "the place for seeing."

The town's theater has recently been rebuilt, replacing creaky old wooden seats with ones of stone. A useful tip for visitors is to take a cushion in with you, as sitting through a long performance on a hard marble seat can be a numbing experience!

Arrive well before the performance begins – not just to get a good seat, but to look around this magnificent building.

Note how the seats are divided into blocks by a horizontal diazoma, or walkway, and by klimakes, or stairways. Each block is known as a kerkis. Wherever you sit, you will have a clear view of the orchestra, or acting area, behind which is the proscenium. This is a low building with a flat roof that actors use as a raised stage. Their dressing rooms, or skene, are behind the stage.

After the play is over, you may find that events are just about to begin at the horse track on the other side of town. Keep up with the crowds!

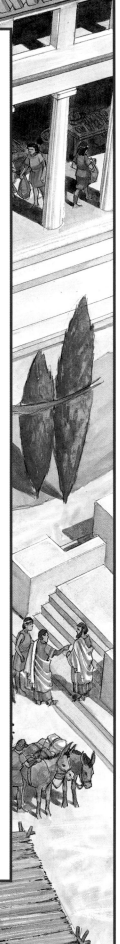

GUIDED TOURS

HORSE TRACK

On race days this is the only place to be in town! The hippodrome will be packed with visitors, there to watch chariots pulled by teams of two or four horses as they race around the track.

The hippodrome is a long rectangle with rounded ends. Tiers of stone seats line the sides. In olden times, spectators sat or stood on grassy banks.

Observe how the course is marked by a tall pillar at either end, around which the chariots must turn. The length of one lap is six stades (about 3,900 feet). The hellanodikai, or judges, arrive at the start of a meeting, robed in purple with garlands on their heads. After they have taken their seats, the chariots and horses pass before them. An official calls out the name of each competitor, his father's name and his city, and asks if anyone has any charge to bring against him. Following this, the chief judge addresses the competitors, and then the racing begins. As many as forty chariots race twelve times around the track.

People bet on who they think will win. The cautious visitor will do well to remember the saying: "A fool and his money are easily parted."

LIGHTHOUSE

It might seem an odd place to visit, but try not to miss out on a tour of the lighthouse. The best time to go is at night, when the fire will be burning in its brazier at the top of the tower.

The lighthouse keeper is pleased to receive visitors, on condition that they help him carry firewood to the top of the tower. Please don't refuse, as to do so will cause offense, and the keeper may not let you enter the building.

Once inside, follow the stone steps as they wind around in a tight spiral up to the fire platform. On the way up you will see small openings in the thick wall, through which you will be able to see how far you have climbed.

Take care at the top. The heat of the raging fire is intense, and more than one visitor has stepped back from the inferno, only to fall over the edge and into the sea far below!

COUNTRYSIDE

The countryside around town is worth a visit. It belongs to the town and is part of what is known as the city-state. The people who live within the area of the city-state are citizens of the town, enjoying the same rights and privileges as their counterparts who live in the town itself.

For your enjoyment, hire a donkey to carry you over the rough tracks that cross the hills and valleys of the district. It may not travel very fast, but its stamina and firm footing will see you safely to your destination. Most people ride side-saddle – if you're not sure, ask someone to show you what to do.

Away from the town, you will soon discover the joys of the Greek countryside. At first you may think the hilly landscape is barren, but you will soon realize the truth is quite different.

Farmers work long hours tending their small fields, growing food to feed the town's population. Is it any wonder that they are highly thought of by their fellow citizens? Note their clothes – hats to protect them from the sun, short tunics that are easy to move in, and leather boots that protect their feet.

GUIDED TOURS TO OTHER PLACES

ATHENS

The great city of Athens should be on the visitor's "must see" list. It owes much of its splendor to one man – the statesman and general Pericles. In 449 B.C. he made peace with the Persians, and the war between Greece and Persia ended. To celebrate, Pericles glorified Athens with new buildings, which you will see.

Take the Panathenaic Way, the road from the city center to the acropolis, on which stands a fine group of temples. Upon entering the sacred enclosure you will come before a large bronze statue of Athena, the goddess of the city. To her right is the Parthenon, the grandest temple of all. Marvel at its 46 columns, each 32 feet tall.

Cross to the Erectheum, the most sacred temple on the hill. Note how some of its columns are carved to look like women. Note also the pool of salt water in a small hollow, made when the god Poseidon struck the rock with his trident.

On the other side of the city is the Pnyx, a hill where the citizens' Assembly meets. Go also to Piraeus, the port, from where you can travel by sea to other parts of Greece. Visitors may go on to Mount Olympus from here, to meet the gods.

MOUNT OLYMPUS

Travel north to Mount Olympus and you will be in the lap of the Olympian gods, as this is where the twelve live:

APHRODITE
goddess of love and beauty
APOLLO
god of truth, music, and healing
ARES
god of war
ARTEMIS
goddess of wild animals
ATHENA
goddess of war, wisdom, and art
DEMETER
goddess of grain and fertility
DIONYSUS
god of wine and vegetation
HERA
goddess of women
HERMES
god of travel, business, and sport
HESTIA
goddess of hearth and home
POSEIDON
god of the sea and earthquakes
ZEUS
god of the weather, king of gods

DELPHI

The sanctuary of the god Apollo is at Delphi, a very holy place. It is said to be the omphalos, meaning navel, the very center of the world.

Delphi lies high on the side of Mount Parnassus, with views across the sea to the Peloponnese, the large part of the mainland which is almost, but not quite, an island.

Pilgrims come to Delphi from all parts of the world, such is its fame. They come seeking answers from the gods to their questions. The priestess of the temple, known as the Pythia, is able to talk to the gods.

The visitor should note that only men are allowed to meet the Pythia – it is only men who can ask a question of the gods. Women must persuade a man to ask a question on their behalf.

Write your question down and hand it to a priest who will be with the Pythia. As he reads it out, you will see the Pythia go into a trance, at which point she asks the gods your question. The strange sounds she utters is the gods' answer, which the priest will translate for you.

A question asked by many visitors is: "Is it safe for me to travel home by sea?" Perhaps this could be your question too.

Glossary

Acropolis Hill at the heart of a Greek town.

Agora Open space used for a town market and business.

Altar Flat-topped block used for offerings to a god.

Amphora Large two-handled storage pot.

Andron Dining room of a house.

Assembly Gathering of the citizens of a city-state.

Aulos Wind instrument, like a flute.

Barbarian Person from a wild, uncivilized tribe.

Bouleuterion Council-house.

Bronze Yellowish metal mixed from copper and tin.

Centaur Mythical creature, part human, part horse creature.

Citizen A free person of a city and its state.

City-state Self-governing city and its land.

Comedy A humorous play.

Council A town's elected officials.

Councillor Member of the council.

Dialect A person's accent.

Discus Stone or metal disc thrown by athletes.

Drachma A coin.

Halter Weight used by athletes in the long jump.

Hippodrome Race track for horses and chariots.

Hoplite Greek foot soldier.

Labyrinth A maze.

Lura Lyre, a musical instrument with strings.

Minotaur Mythical creature, part human, part bull living in the Labyrinth.

Obol A coin.

Olympian One of the twelve gods on Mount Olympus.

Orchestra The performing area of a theater.

Ostracism Process of sending a person into exile.

Rhapsode Storyteller who tells stories in a poetic way.

Sanctuary A holy place.

Siege When an army keeps people trapped in their town.

Stade Unit of length, equal to about 650 feet (200 meters).

Stele Stone marker, often put by a grave.

Stoa Low building with columns and shops inside.

Stoics Group of thinkers who believe in one god, not many.

Styx River between the worlds of the living and the dead.

Symposium Drinking party for men only.

Temenos Sacred enclosure in which stands a temple.

Tragedy A sad play.

Trance A sleep-like state.

Trireme Greek warship.

Underworld Where people's spirits go after death.

INDEX